Flag Day

By Kelly Bennett

Consultant
Nanci R. Vargus, Ed.D.
Assistant Professor
Literacy Education
University of Indianapolis
Indianapolis, Indiana

Children's Press®
A Division of Scholastic Inc.
New York   Toronto   London   Auckland   Sydney
Mexico City   New Delhi   Hong Kong
Danbury, Connecticut

Designer: Herman Adler Design
Photo Researcher: Caroline Anderson
The photo on the cover shows children celebrating Flag Day.

Library of Congress Cataloging-in-Publication Data

Bennett, Kelly.
  Flag Day / by Kelly Bennett.
    p. cm. — (Rookie read-about holidays)
Includes index.
Summary: Presents a simple introduction to the traditions and
festivities on Flag Day including basic flag etiquette.
  ISBN 0-516-22862-5 (lib. bdg.)   0-516-27755-3 (pbk.)
  1. Flag Day—Juvenile literature. [1. Flag Day. 2. Holidays.] I.
Title. II. Series.
  JK1761 .B46 2003
  394.263—dc21
                                    2002015126

3 1984 00239 3880

It is Flag Day. Let's sing
"Happy Birthday" to
the flag!

The United States flag is a symbol of our country.

We fly it to show that we are Americans.

There was no "United States" in the early 1700s. Instead, there were thirteen American colonies ruled by England.

The Americans thought the English king was unfair. They wanted to be their own rulers.

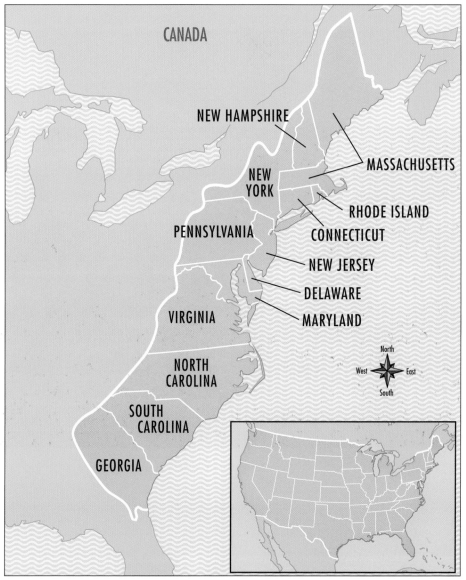

The thirteen colonies in 1776

In 1776, Americans formed a new nation. They called it the United States of America.

They fought a war to become free from England.

During the war, different American groups flew different flags. Some had rattlesnakes, pine trees, or other symbols.

Some leaders thought it was confusing to have so many flags.

They thought all Americans should fly the same flag.

June 2003

Sunday	Monday	Tuesday	Wednesday	Thursday	Friday	Saturday
1	2	3	4	5	6	7
8	9	10	11	12	13	14
15	16	17	18	19	20	21
22	23	24	25	26	27	28
29	30					

On June 14, 1777,
American leaders chose
the first national flag.

That is why we celebrate
Flag Day on June 14.
It is the flag's birthday.

The first United States flag had thirteen stripes for the thirteen colonies. It had thirteen stars, too.

Over the years, the flag changed. Every time a new state joined the nation, the flag got a new star.

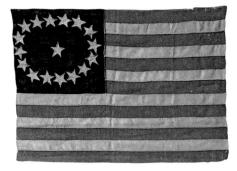
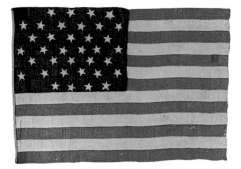
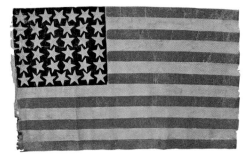
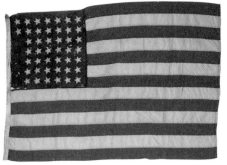

Today the flag has fifty
stars for fifty states.

On Flag Day, towns have parades or gatherings. People wave flags and sing.

You may hear "Stars and Stripes Forever" or "The Star Spangled Banner."

19

We say the Pledge of Allegiance on Flag Day.

We stand, face the flag, and put our right hands over our hearts.

When we say the pledge, we are promising to honor our flag and our country.

There are many rules about how to treat the flag.

It must never touch the ground.

The flag should be hung with the blue square in the top, left-hand corner.

When an American flag
is flown with other flags,
it belongs at the top of
the flagpole.

Many people fly flags only
from sunrise to sunset. A
flag flying at night should
be well lit.

A flag that is not being used should be folded in a neat triangle.

We honor our flag and our country on Flag Day.

Hooray for the Red, White and Blue!

Words You Know

colonies

flagpole

parade

Pledge of Allegiance

stars

stripes

symbol

triangle

31

Index

About the Author

Kelly Bennett has written six books for children. She likes to have adventures with her son Max and her daughter Alexis. She lives in Katy, Texas.

Photo Credits